Relax. Nothing is under control.
Adi Da

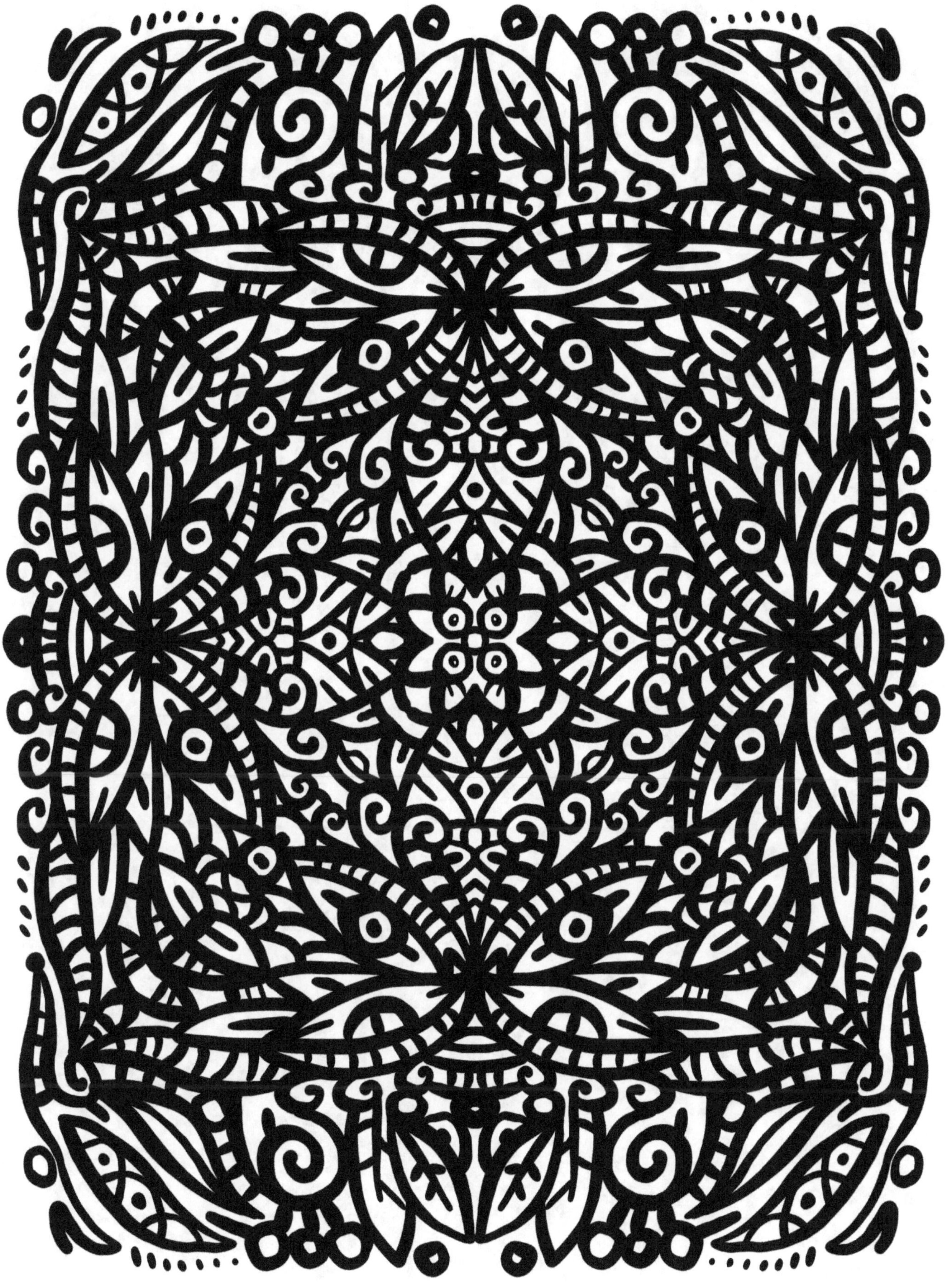

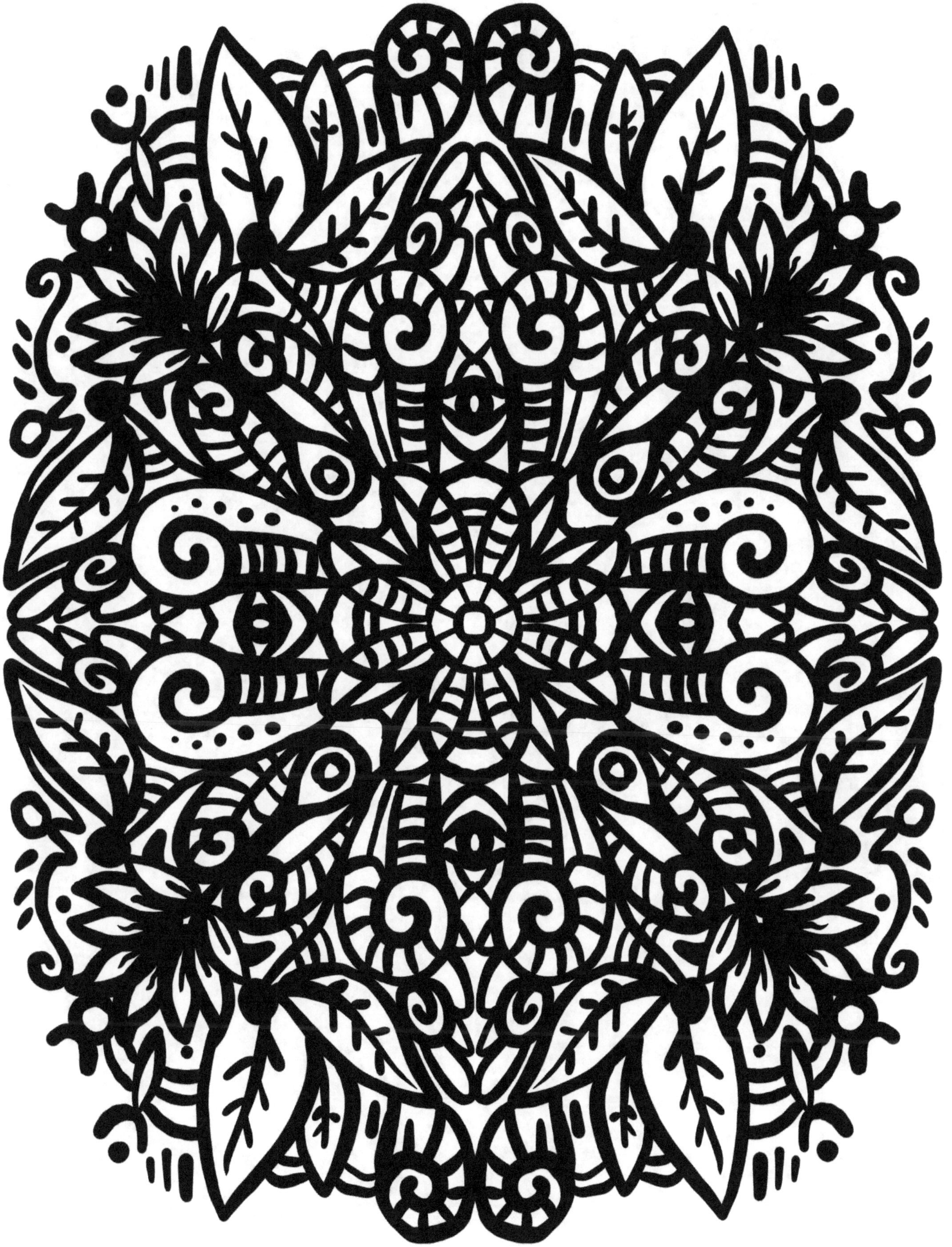

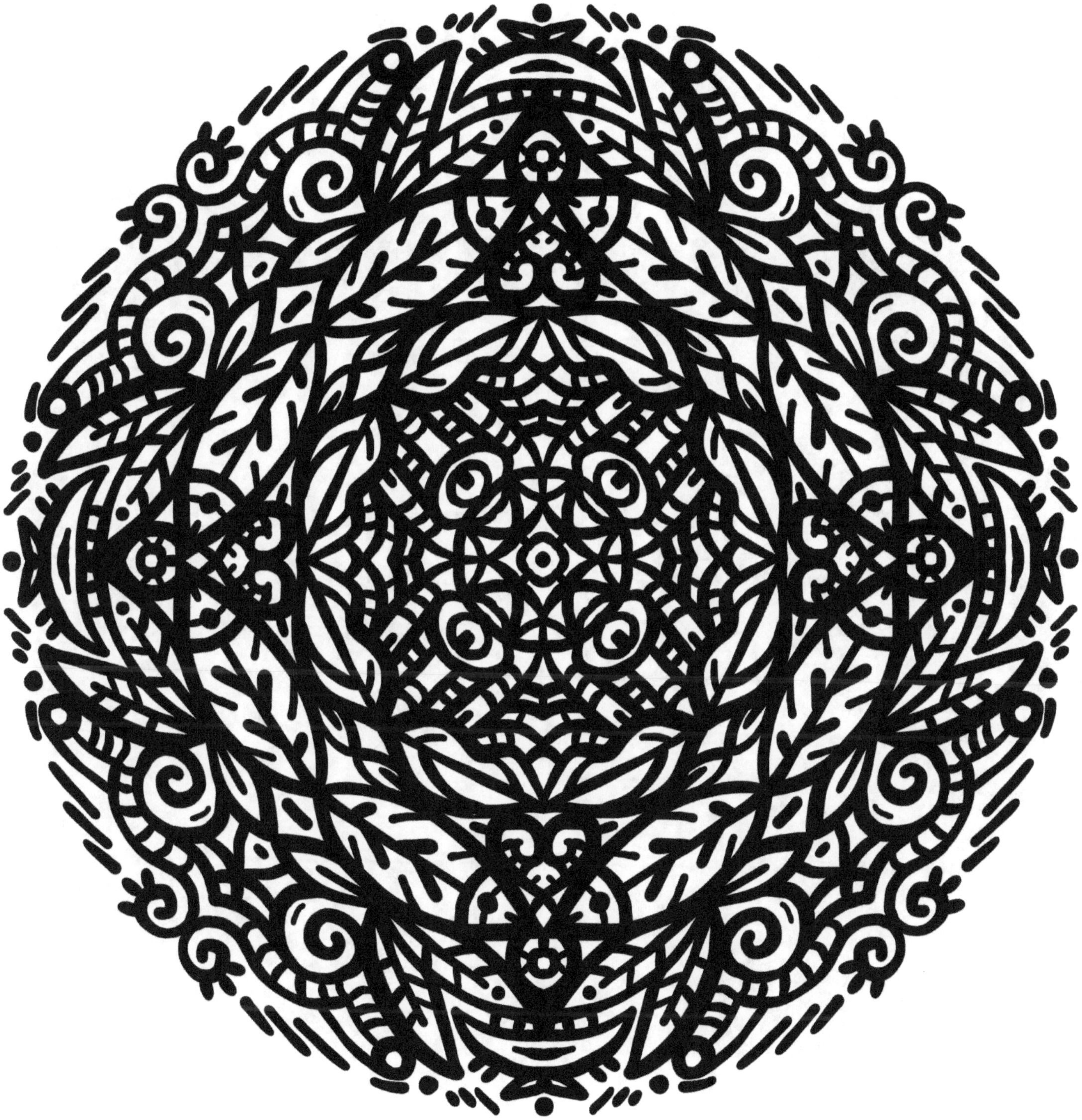

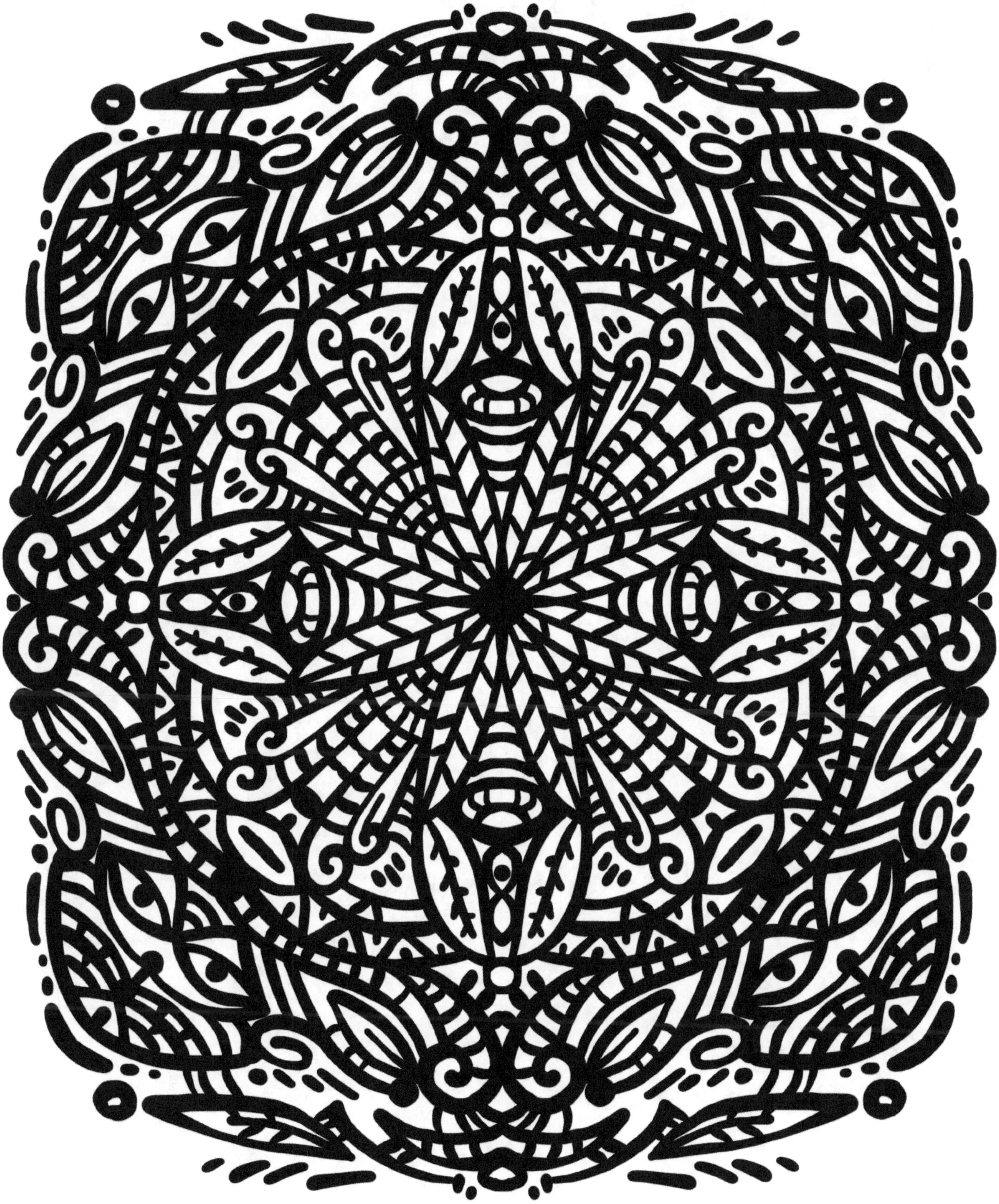

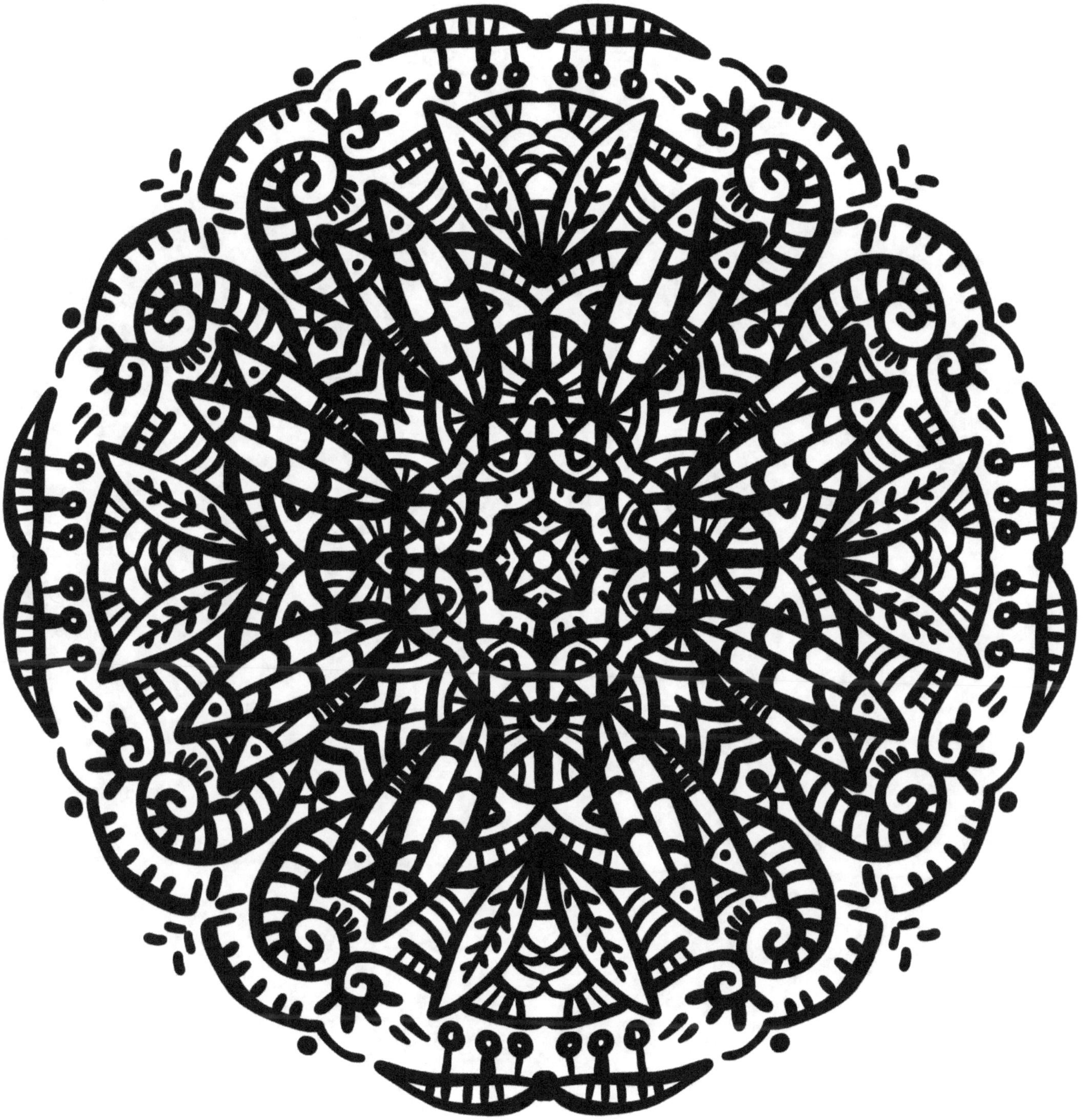

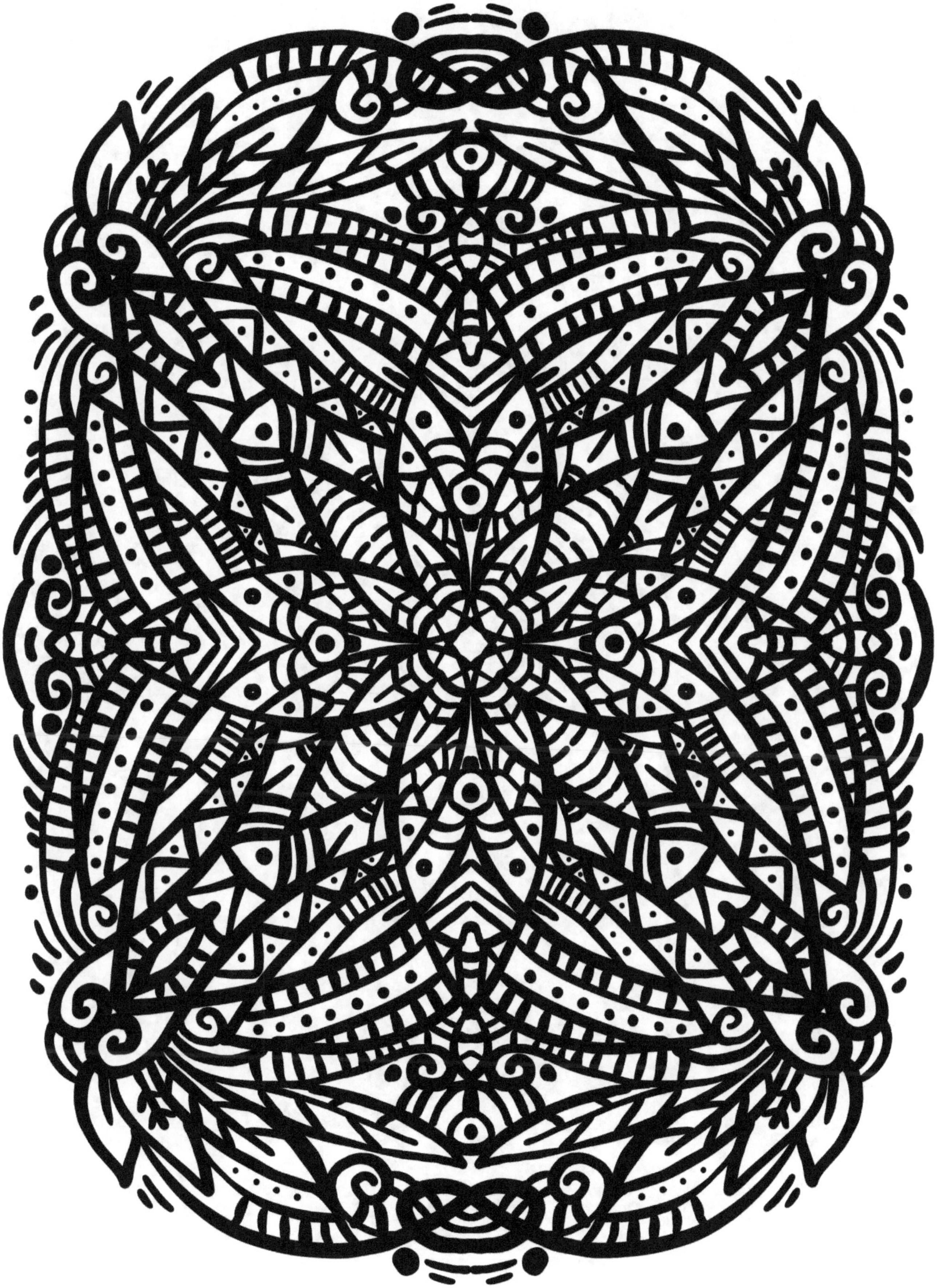

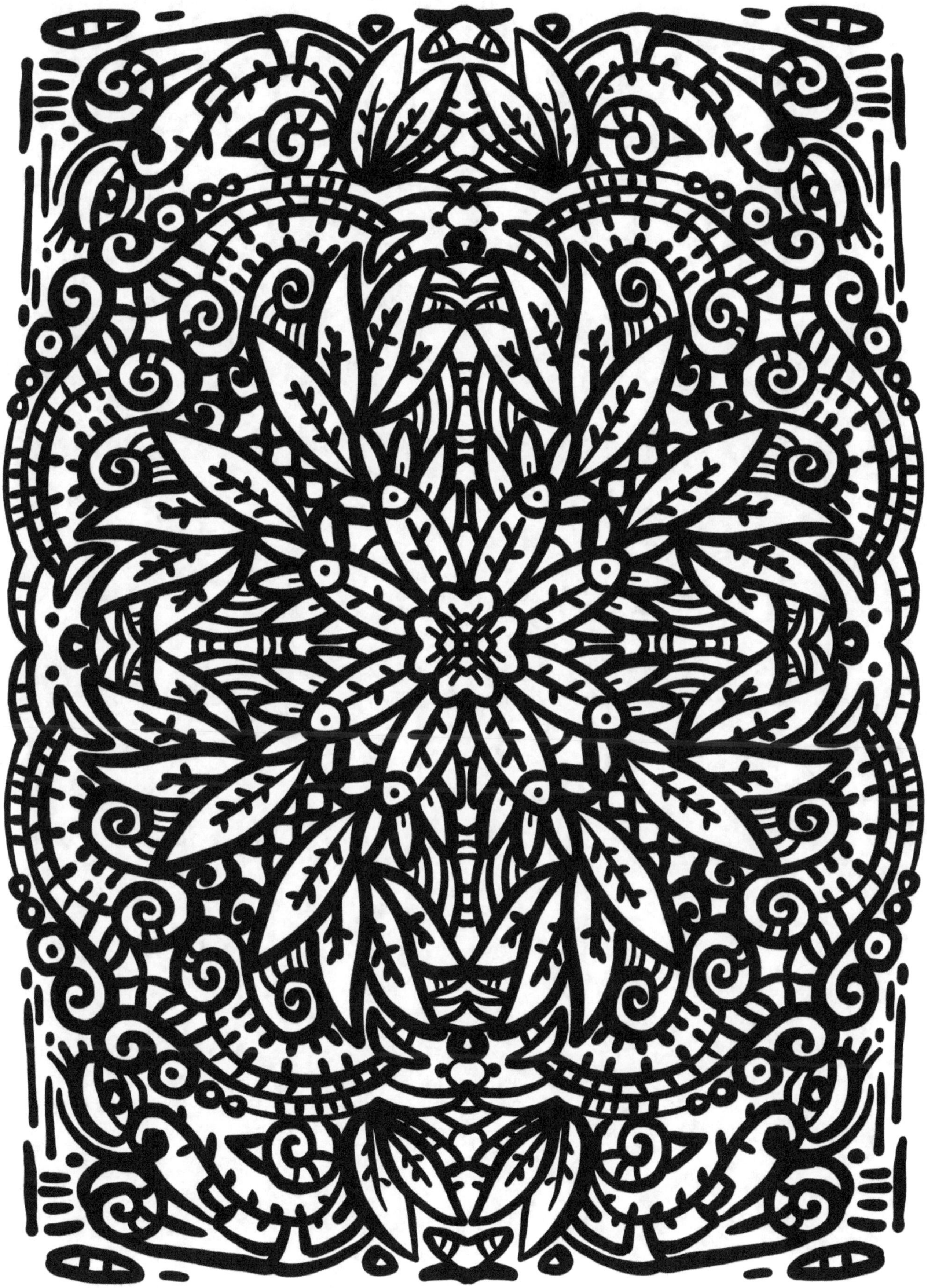

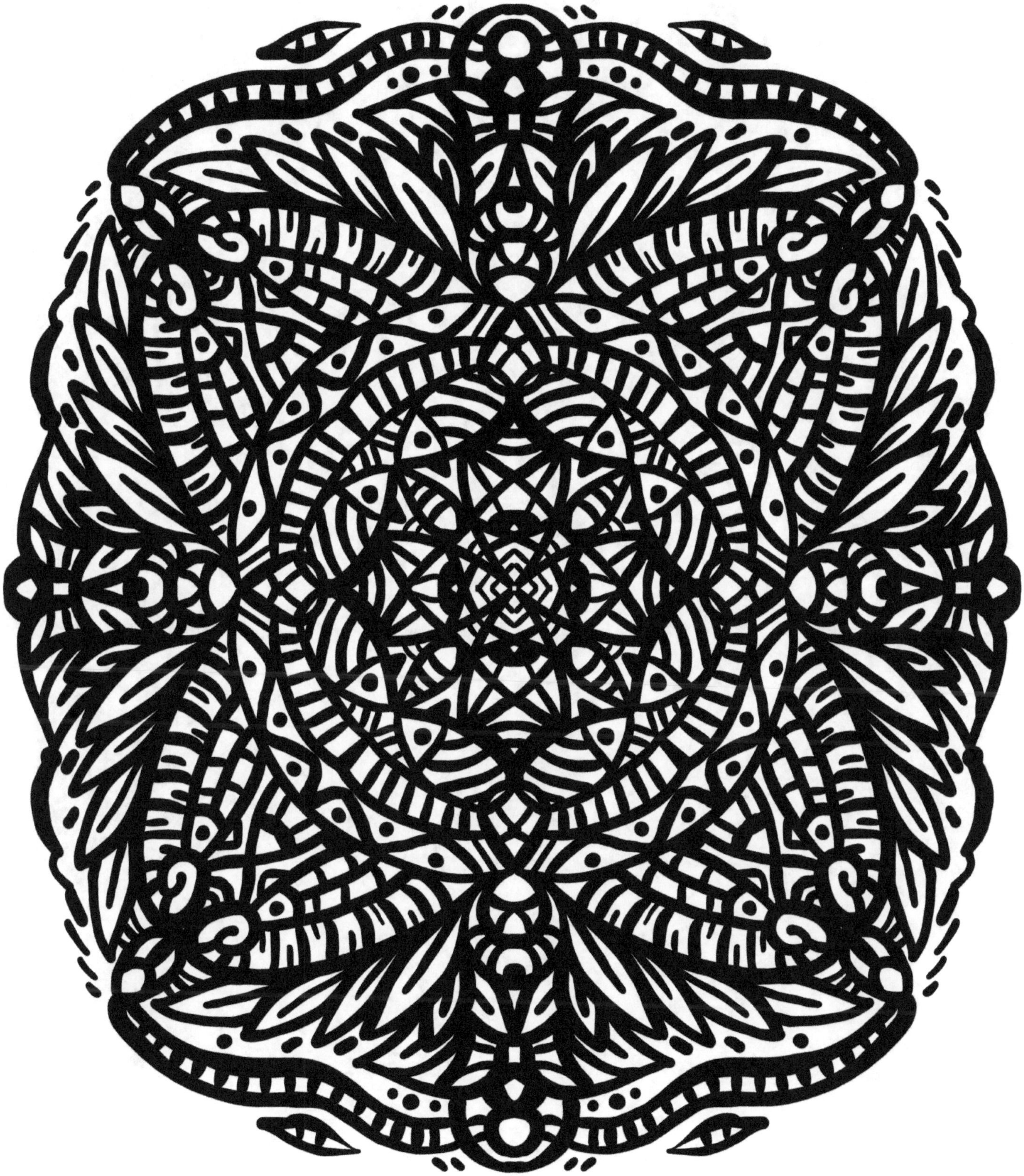

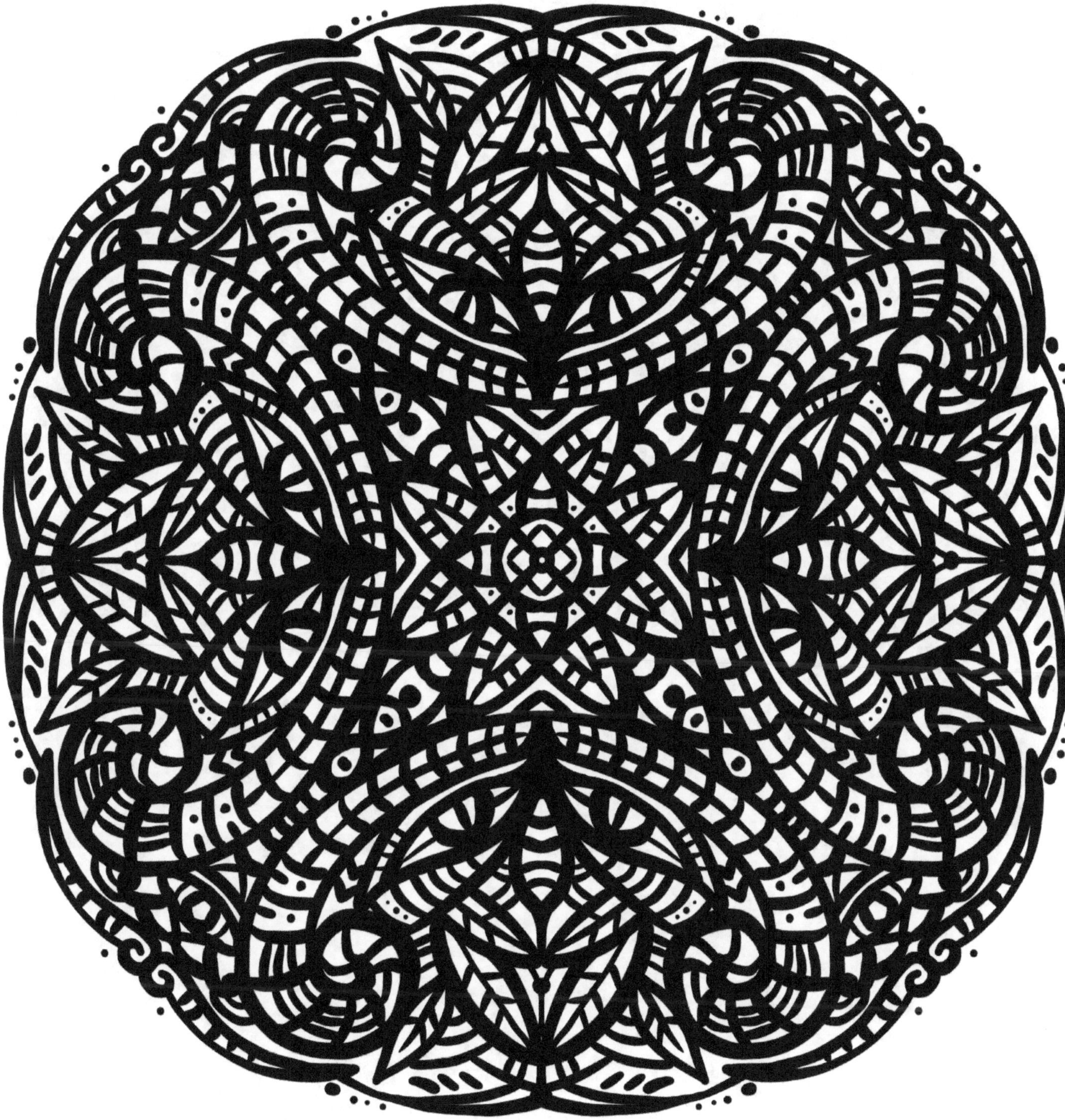

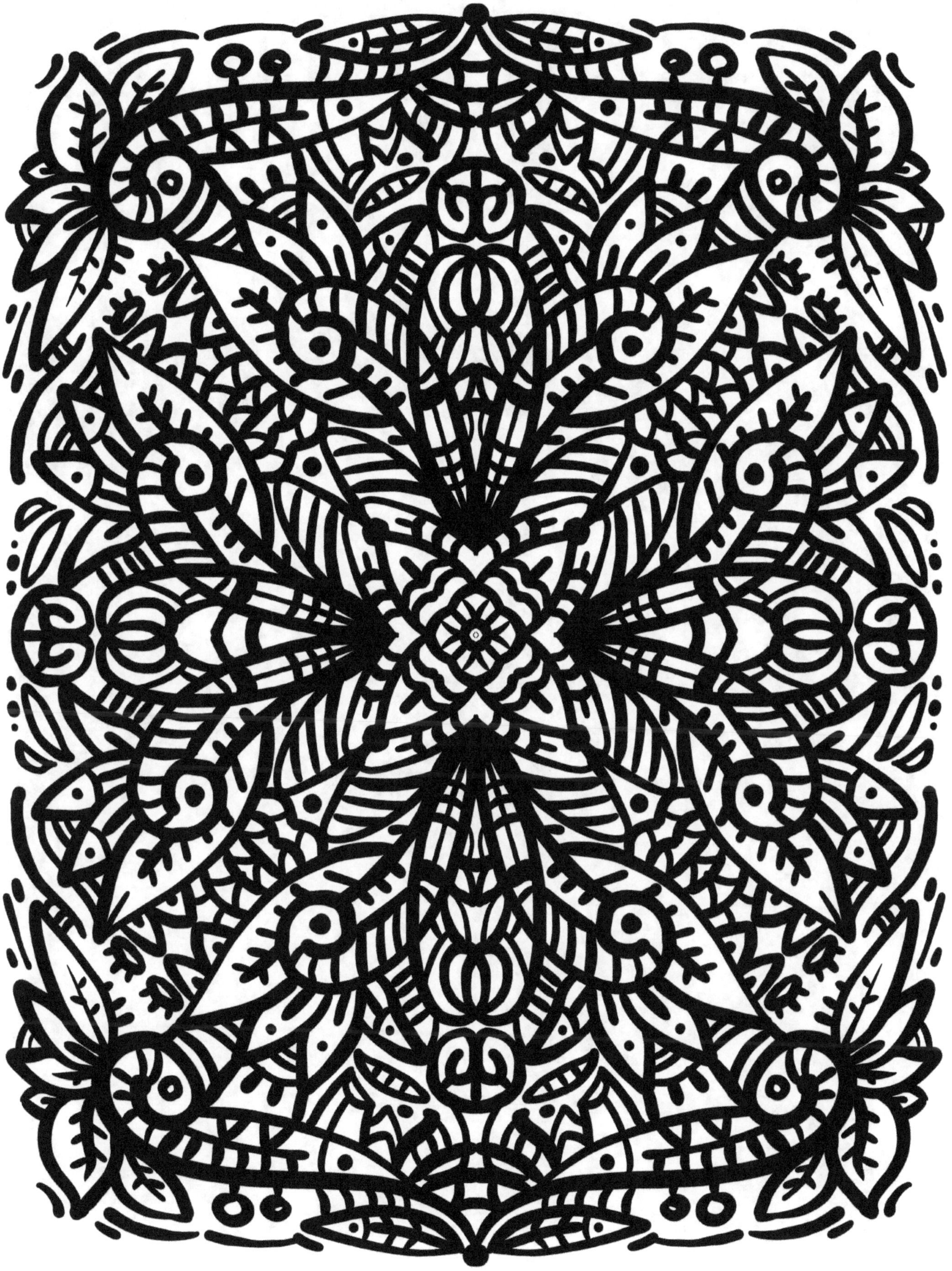

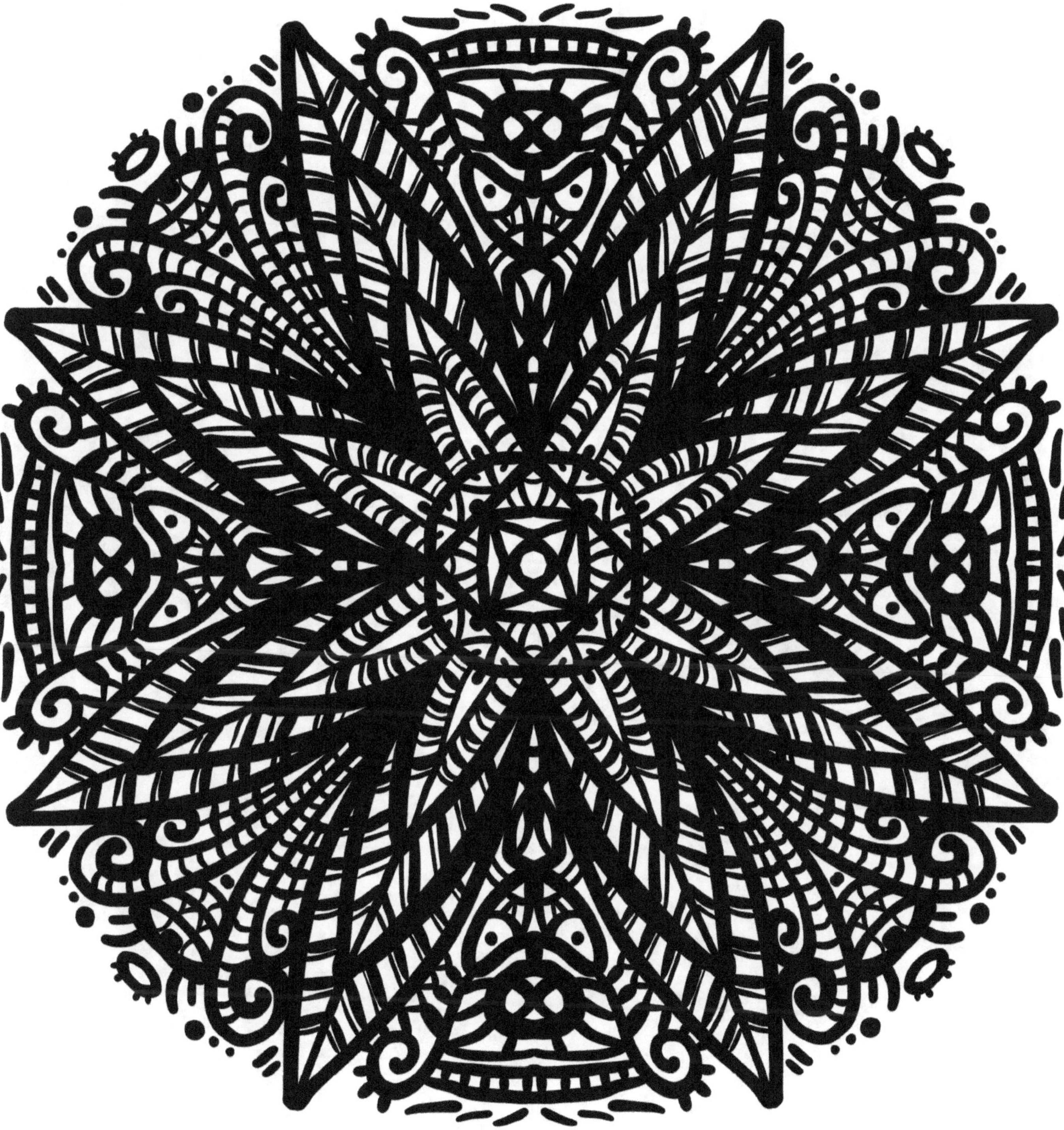

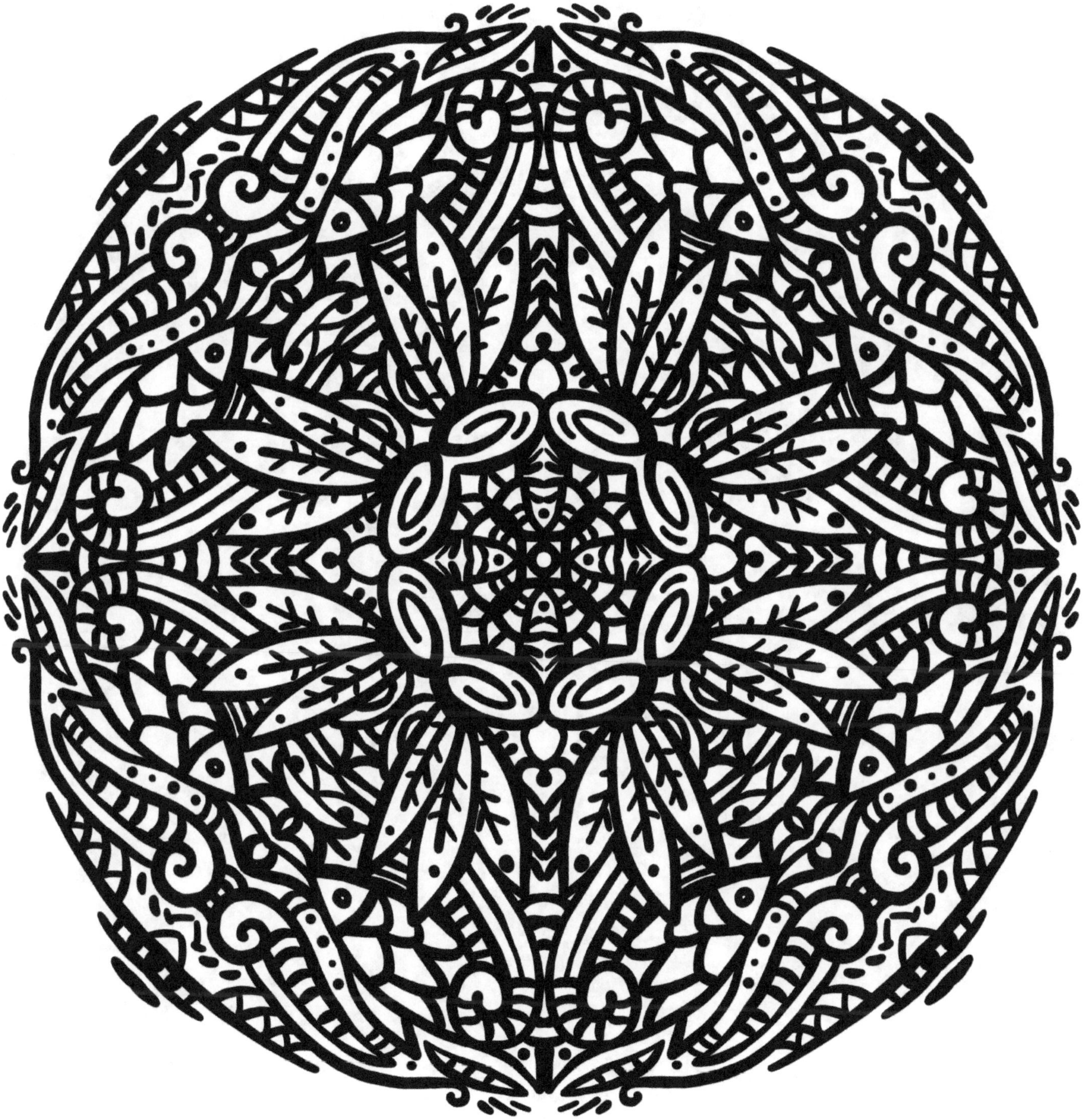

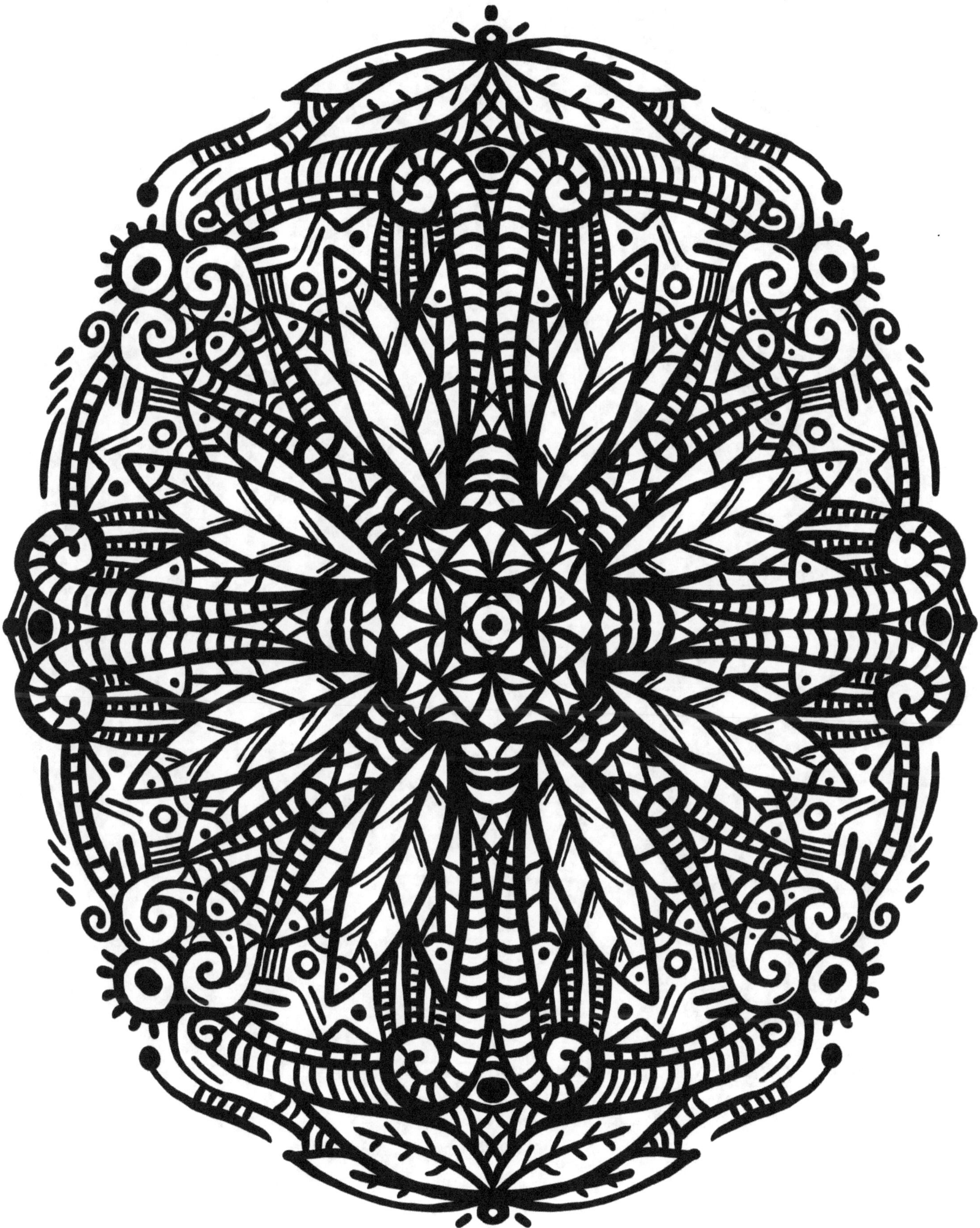

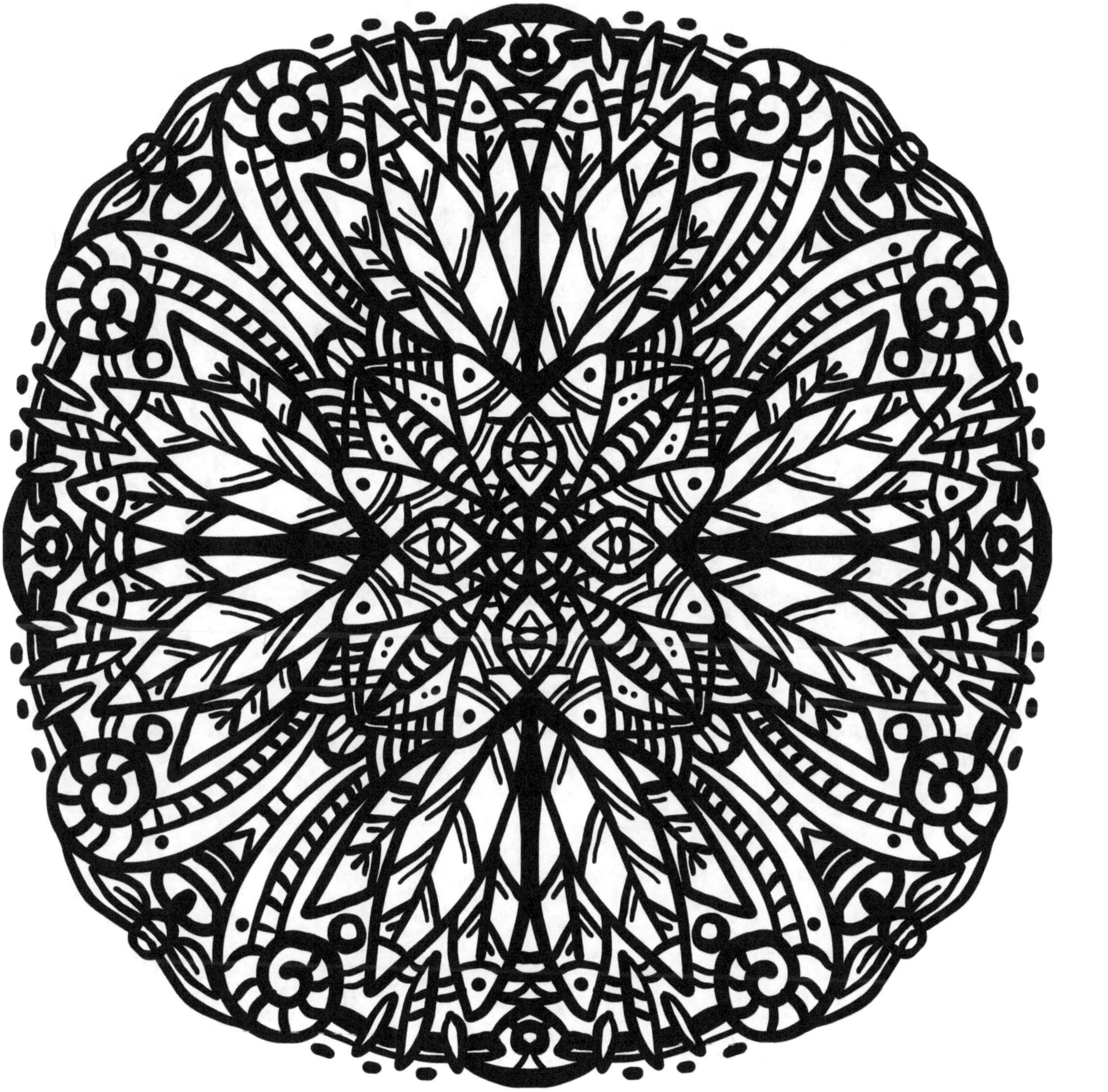

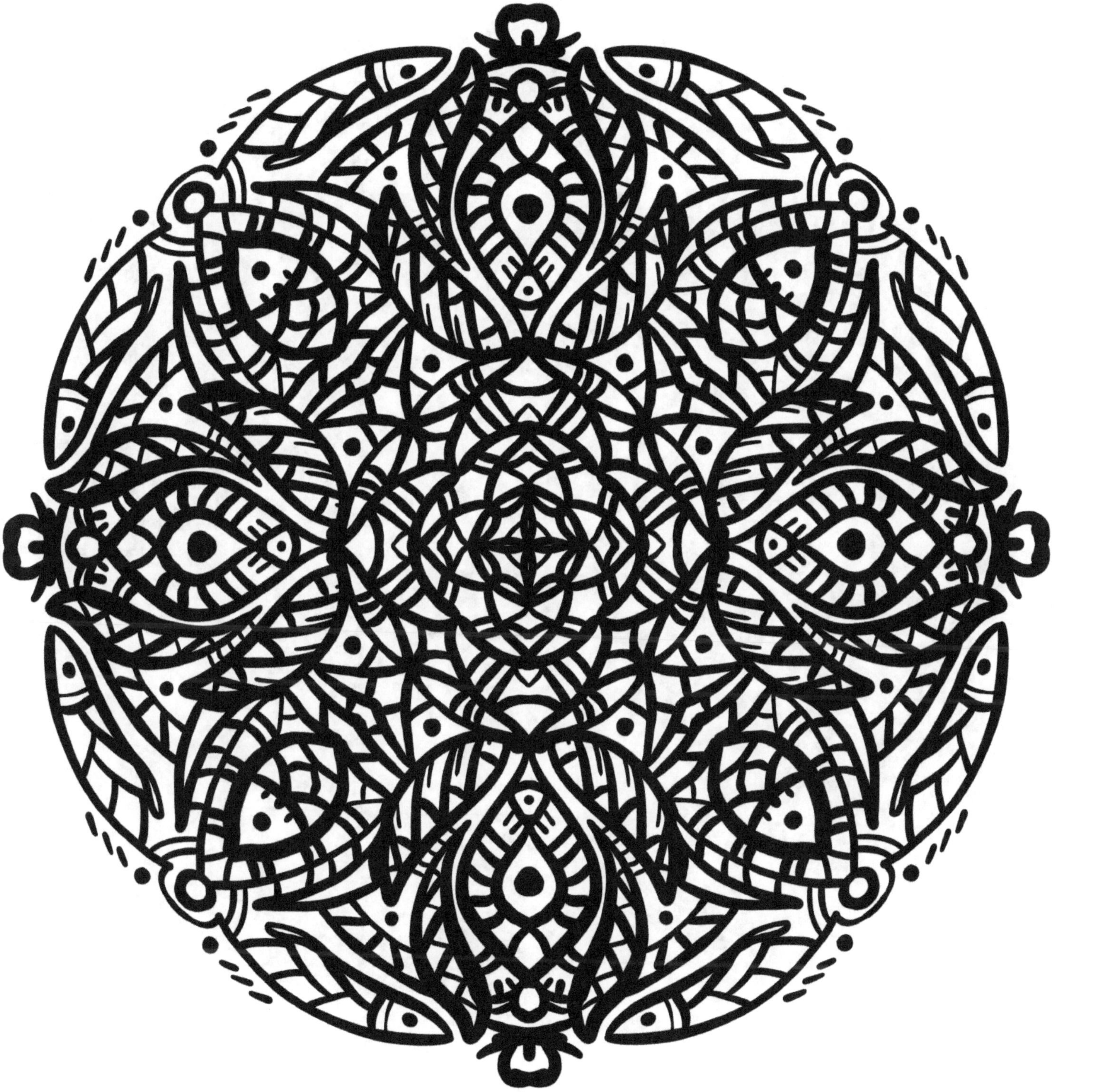

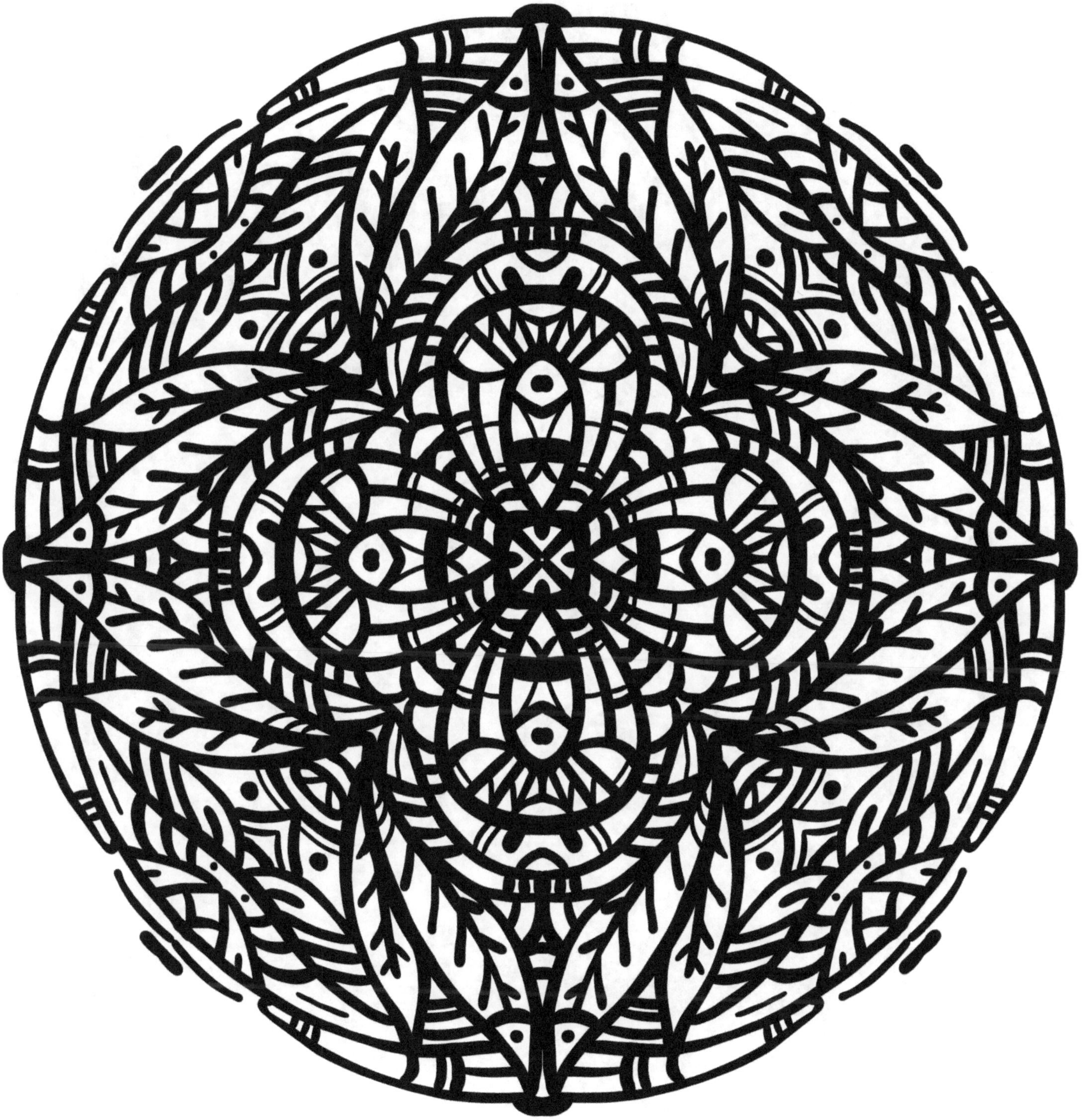

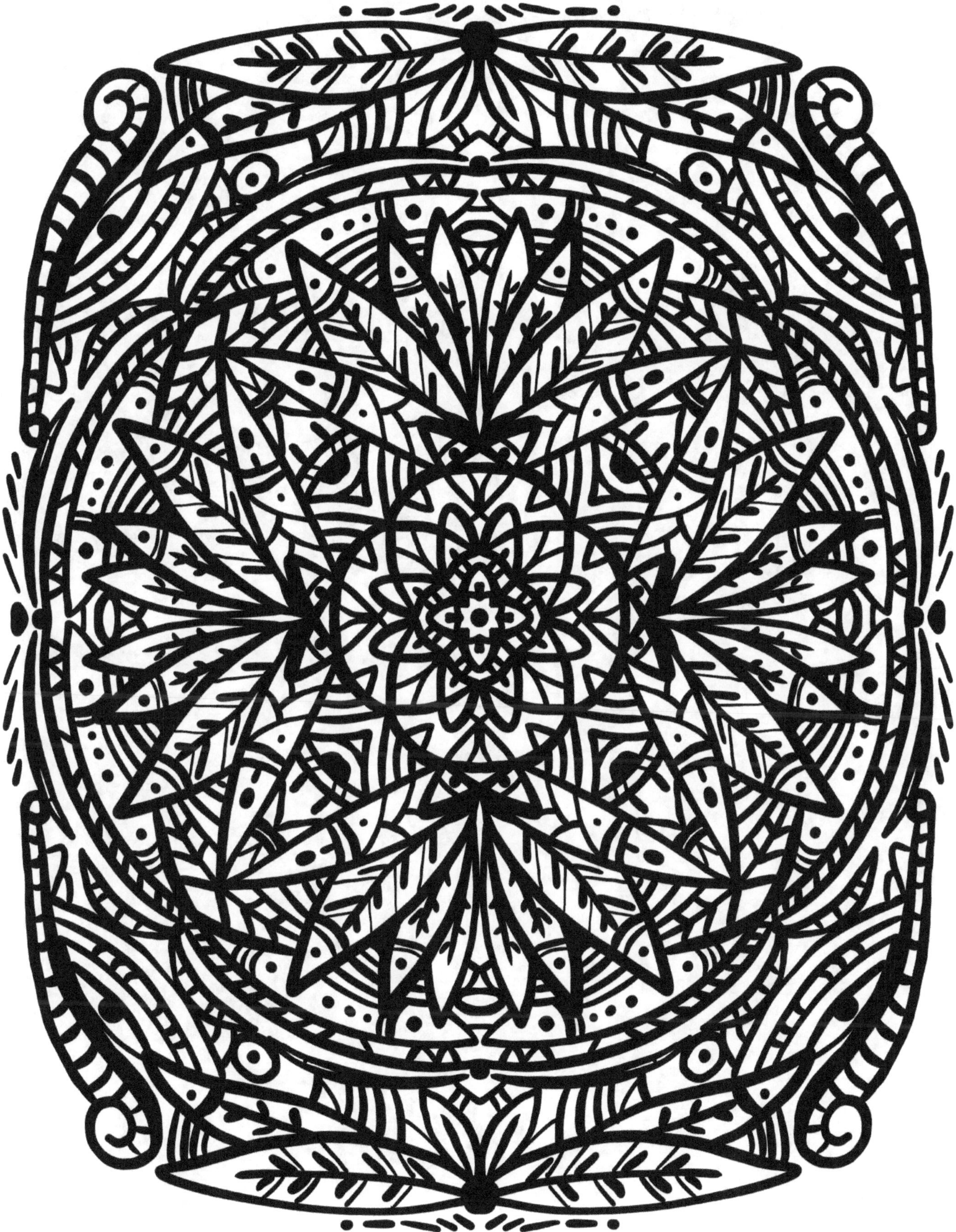

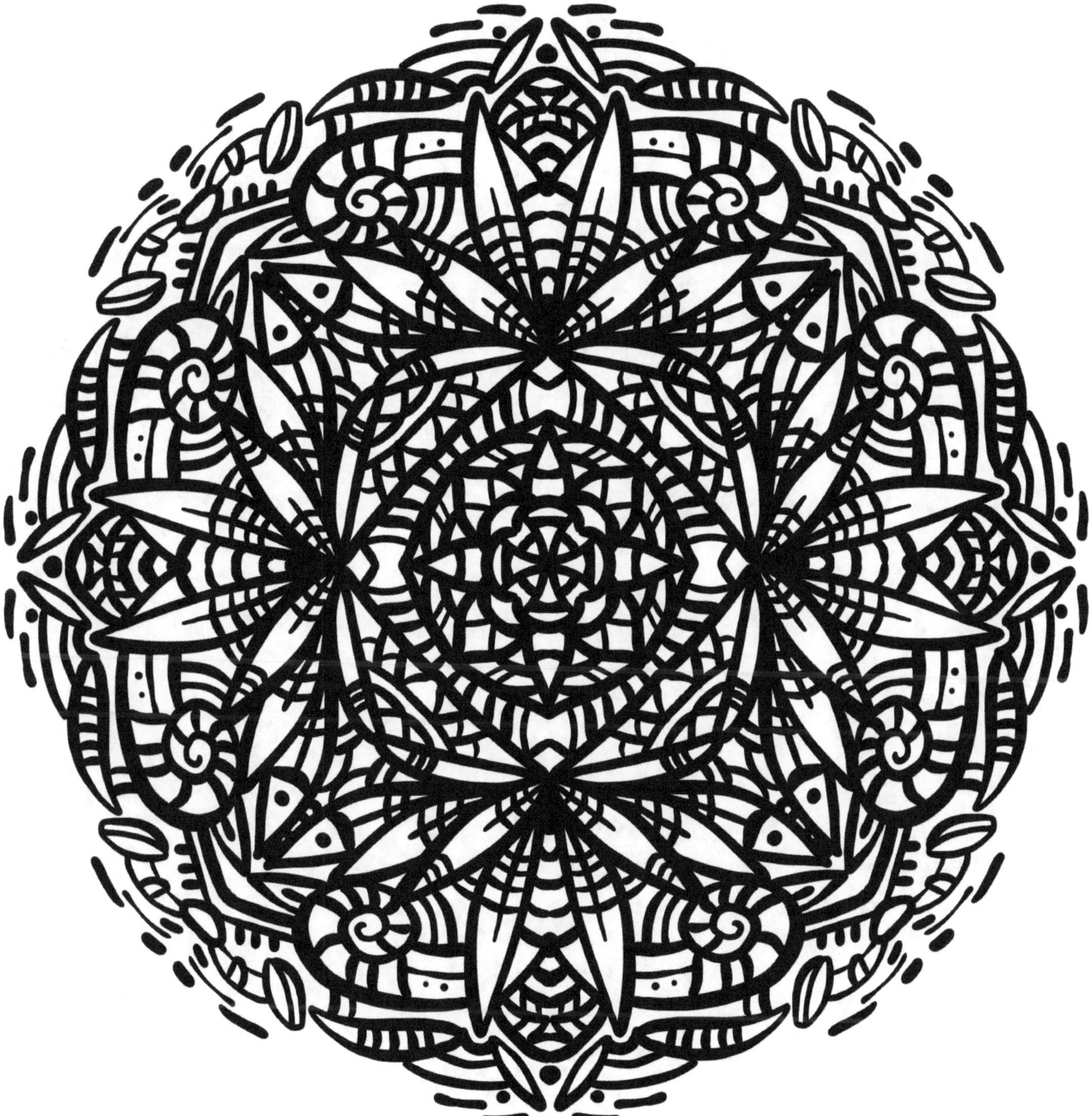

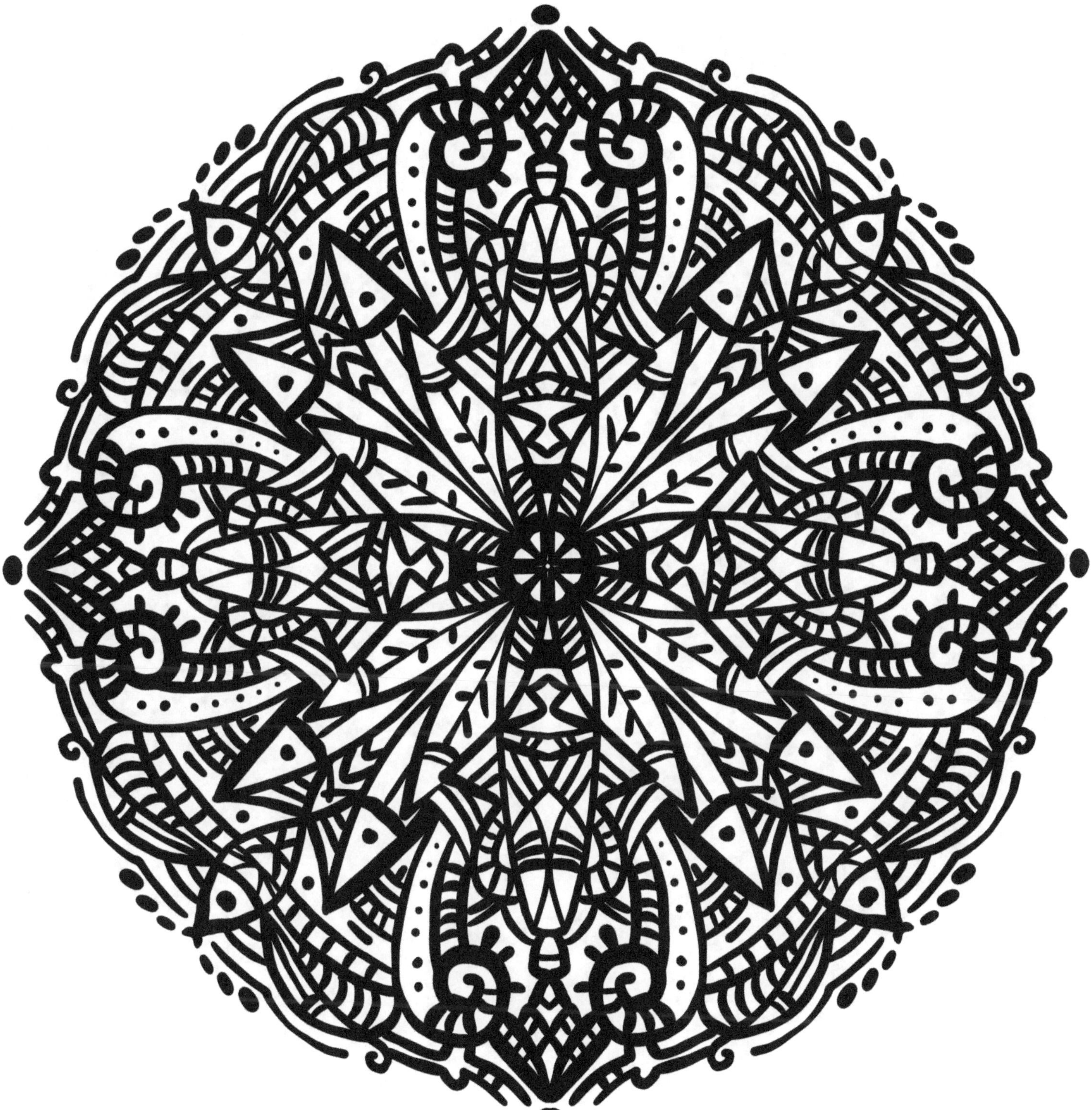

www.ingramcontent.com/pod-product-compliance
Lightning Source LLC
Chambersburg PA
CBHW080628220526
45467CB00011B/3418